The Evolution Of Love.

a collection of poetry by **L'MAY.**

THE EVOLUTION OF LOVE

Copyright © 2024 by L'May

All rights reserved.
No part of this book may be reproduced, or stored in a retrieval system, or transmitted in any form or by any means, electronic, mechanical, photocopying, recording, or otherwise, without express written permission of the publisher.

Book Layout and Illustrations by: Rein G.
www.fiverr.com/reindrawthings

One truth remains universal: Lessons are only meaningful if you learn from them, & heartbreaks are most appreciated once you heal. Those who have journeyed through the evolution of love will have encountered both the joy & the pain.
This collection explores different facets & perspectives of love, sparking reflection rather than direct understanding.

She wanted to live life with
No regrets.
Leave —
No word left unsaid.

Love so deep &
Hold nothing back.
Find strength in her weakest moments.

This bucket list
Was not for the faint hearted.

COLLECTION:

YOUNG 1

TOXIC 15

A NARCISSIST'S LOVE 35

BEST-FRIEND? 51

FOREVER 65

YOUNG

Adjective: a naïve, innocent stage of life, unready to be shaped by the experiences ahead.

1. The two were inseparable, young love at it's finest.

2. They were young and their emotions' heightened.

Noun (plural): Young people.

Meeting You.

From the moment my eyes met yours.

To every second in your presence.

Every joke exchanged
Every glance
Every touch.

We were completely unaware
That we were one step closer —
To falling in love.

Falling.

His warm smile,
His awkward laugh.

Our nervous encounters,
Our anxious hearts.

He's perfectly imperfect.
Beautifully made from head to toe.

Utterly cliché
But
So is LOVE.

Fate.

Is he the one?
Then let it be.

What is made for me shall be.

100 Butterflies.

The bell rings.
I jump to pack my books away,
Feeling a light spark in my chest,
Hoping that I might see you.

Luckily I'm by the door,
Amongst the first to leave the room,
Fixing my skirt & shirt,
As if you care.
'But it's the little things, right?'

I can see past the people in front of me,
Your classroom door opens.

I try not to get my hopes up,
I try to appear blissfully unaware.

As I get to the front of the queue,
I catch a glimpse of what might be you.

It is you.

We lock eyes —
My stomach flips,
My heart stops
& I feel 100 butterflies.

All in that one moment.

You smile as I call your name,
I feel elated —
As you wrap your arm around my shoulders.

We walk to my next class
& innocently lock hands as we wait by the door.

Seconds pass…
You promise me you'll get to your class on time.

I fall back into reality
Once you're gone.

Completely caught off guard by
What just happened.

My mind goes on to replay
Those short-lived moments
Until the bell rings.

Unfamiliar.

It was a weird time.

Everything felt,
Everything smelt,
Looked? Unfamiliar.

Lighter,
Brighter,
Simpler.

& you were terribly different
To what I had imagined,
It felt special, you choosing me.

Every time summer comes around,
I'm reminded of you.

What a weird & special time.

Yin & Yang.

It was love at first sight,
Yin & yang beautifully contrasting,
Their effervescent flames flickered bright,
Their love was to be everlasting...

Nothing pure seems to last in this society,
An innocent heart can soothe a tortured soul.
But at the price of selflessness in its entirety,
Therefore these two hearts cannot stay whole.

A magnetic attraction,
All that consumes them is passion,
Resistance to let go is their reaction,
As nothing else in this world —
Can meet their satisfaction.

LOVE was not enough,
For this to work.
Selflessness had to become selfishness.

Gone was that spark.

Impulse.

Why when everything is so perfect,
Do
We have the URGE to
Mess
It
All
Up?

Forewarning.

A harsh reality,
That heartbreak
Feels almost mandatory.

Like some sort of sick rite of passage,
In order to *find your true love.*

Do we warn the innocent hearts?

That one day,
"Someone you think
Loves you more than you deserve —
Might lie to you,
Hurt you,
Play with your feelings.
Tell you that you're their
'Favourite human',
Meanwhile treat that other person,
That you repeatedly ask & worry about,
Like they are their absolute world.
(Behind closed doors, of course).

The good days make you feel like
It's all worth it.
But your heart knows —

That this love is
Oh
So
Temporary.

You'll fight to make it last longer than it should,
Whilst you pray for the days —
That you can call this
A distant memory."

If you had this beauty of hindsight,
Would you choose differently...

Should we warn them?

Nah.

TOXIC

Adjective: *(Poisonous)* A relationship that leads you down a euphoric rollercoaster. Leaves you feeling perturbed, empty, numb — but more than anything, craving more. One can often become addicted to the cyclical pattern of juxtaposing emotions.

1. I know this is toxic, but I just can't leave...

2. A love this toxic should be bottled and sold to the highest bidder, at least then you'll know it was highly sought after. I didn't want this.

Delulu.

I say I don't need closure,
I say I don't care anymore.

What can I say?

My coping mechanism is delusion.

Out of Sight,
Out of mind,
They say.

How about:
Delete, block, thank you, next.

If only that was it.

Hindsight.

We told each other we loved each other,
But your words didn't match your actions.

Ironically, neither did mine.

I wish I handled things differently,
I was wrong & you were blind.

I guess we were both immature,
It's nothing that couldn't be fixed with time.

I know you weren't right for me,
& yet I still chose to ignore the signs.

Perception.

She fell in love with a false reality,
& it was all that she could see.

He showed her
Time & time again,
But denial chose
Who she wanted him to be.

In her eyes, the good outweighed the bad.

I guess love truly overpowers hate.

Unmet.

Why do we want to change something that we love?

Nothing is perfect,
Even if we want it to be.

Hope.

Patiently waiting,
On the brink of pure joy.

Whilst my head fights my emotions,
Reminding me that there is a chance of —
Disappointment.

The phone rings!
This time could be different?

My heart sinks to the bottom of my stomach,
As the familiar lump returns to the back
Of my throat.

I throw my coat on the floor &
Collapse by the wall.

You'd think I'd be used to this —
Maybe next time will be different.

Choices.

I'd rather be around you - hurting,
Than without you - healing.

That's when I knew this was toxic.

You'd rather keep me trapped - hoping
Than let us both go - knowing.

That's when you knew this was toxic.

& yet we still could not say goodbye.

Secrets.

When you start to lie to those around you,
The secrecy may heighten the pleasure.

Although you often forget,
How much it also heightens the pain.

When you're left alone with that
Familiar heartache,
Having to keep a brave face to conceal the shame.

Every *'we're over now'* is met with a sigh or
An eye roll — no one believes you.

All because of him.

You wish with your whole heart that you
Could hate him.

Maybe that would make it easier to leave
This kind of love behind.

A Mystery.

Growing is knowing that things were not always
As they seemed.

I know that you weren't made for me,
Your cut, your perspective,
Your love was not made for me.
We did not fit, but I forced it &
Hurt us both in the process.

Gave you a false sense of security,
Luring you to places that
You hated as your bruises shone brighter
Than any diamond,
Your words echoed as if we were always
In empty spaces.

You were only safe with me,
When the world would fall away &
It was just you & I.

We existed in only two places —
Spaces that were hidden
From those around us.

That's not love, nor was it lust.
You were a constant mystery that I longed
To uncover.
The truth would be found,
Our wounds had time to heal.
But then we would pick at it over & over.

I felt like a villain in my own love story.

Once that mystery faded
So did said 'love'
Once the mystery was gone,
So were you.

The safe spaces eventually revealed themselves —
To be dirty rooms,
With broken padlocks on every door.

We were trapped in a maze,
That only you could free us from.

So thank you & I'm sorry.

You weren't so bad after all.

One Day.

Some days you can forget
& then some days you can't.

Lucid Dream.

The deep ache,
From the centre of your chest
To the pit of your stomach.

Everything you touch, smell, hear, see
Triggers a memory.

You close your eyes to forget,
Only to be woken up by the lingering
Pain in your heart,
Reminding you that
It. Is. Over.

What was once yours,
Is now no longer.

As you fall through the realms of memories,
You yearn for this to be reality,
Knowing that as soon as you wake up —
It's. Still. Over.

What was once yours,
Is now no longer.

But,
This too shall pass.

Longing.

Does that ache
In your chest
Ever go away?

Plot twist —
No.

Clarity.

This time felt different.

The boy she thought she knew;
Whose touch & smell
Once felt familiar.
Whose presence
Once brought her comfort & happiness.
Whose words
Once permeated her every emotion.

This time she felt nothing.
A complete stranger full of
Deceit, tired effort & sadness.

The rose tint had shattered.
This time was the last time.
They were finally over...

Rhetoric.

You remind me of my past—
Which I shall not entertain for 2 reasons:

I grew the most
Once I left my colourful past behind.

I'm likely to choose you
Over every other priority
I'm likely to believe all of your lies.

That kind of love was toxic,
That kind of person would leave me out to dry.

I'm wise enough to know now,
Despite —
Being young enough to still waste time.

Therefore, our meaningless connection —
Is not something I'll be entertaining,
I refuse to cross that line.

My time will be filled with great loves,
My next one will be divine.

Apologies,
That was more than 2 reasons —
I'm sure you can understand why.

Amnesia.

There are months where you don't cross
My mind or midst.

I forget —
About our memories,
I forget about you.

I let slip —
How you made me feel
In the moments we once shared.

& then —
I hear that one song,
Walk by that familiar scent
& it all comes flooding back.

Washing over me from head to toe.
My hairs begin to stand tall,
As my heart crawls into my stomach.

I do nothing.
Knowing that this feeling,
Is as close to you as I'll ever be.

If I had the choice, would I shake off these
Sporadic moments?

Maybe not.

A NARCISSIST'S LOVE

A person who deems their love for others and themselves as somewhat superior. Their loved ones may become a causality of their thoughtless, selfish actions. They often attempt to consume as many self-satisfying relationships to appease their bottomless egos.

1. A narcissist's love feels one sided.
2. A narcissist's love interest is often a hopeless romantic who perpetually falls in love with potential.

Jekyll & Hyde.

I love with one side,
I hate with the other.

Ego.

Love is a game
Where we all lose.

I want you to fall for me,
For me to feel safe & secure
In the fake promises & false comfort
That I create for you.

All in the hope that I protect my heart.

Because logic must override emotion
& all I'm left with, is me.

I love you but I choose sanity.

With sanity, I choose
Me.

Sensation-Seeking.

In a game where I could lose everything,
In the hope that I gain the greatest high.

I choose you & this;
To let myself fall.

Fall into you,
Wholeheartedly.

Allow myself to be victim to emotion,
Inspired by you, my muse.

The constant what-if,
After every elation you bring.

You have control of this journey.

As petrified as I am,
You are worthy of the fall?

You spark my highest highs &
Conduct my lowest lows.

My addiction has turned into reliance,
As my craving has turned into dependence.

I will fall over & over again,
To feel that high.

To feel you.

Half-Empty.

Your words appear
To be a glass jar filled
With everything
That I could possibly want.

You keep pouring
&
pouring
&
pouring.

I'm so close to taking
It all in.

Persistence is not consistence.

Soon that jar will be empty.

Half-Full.

Heartbreak
Can often make a person appreciate
When their heart feels whole.

Denialist.

Accepting the truth,
& reminiscing has led me to open a door that
I cannot seem to close.

What's the point in healing,
If you can't get over the trauma.

Yes, I'd rather be in denial,
& remain blissfully unaware.

You may have affected me,
But not as much as I'd like to admit or care.

Subdued.

She chooses love over
Hate.
Forgiveness over
Anger.

With that comes a world of pain.

She chooses to endure life
Subdued by its perpetual lows,
To exist only —
For the rarest of sovereign highs.

Temptation.

I crave attention —
Often.

Sometimes —
I want someone to fulfil my every desire.

I want it to be *you*.
& if not you —
I get scared.

Scared that my love for you one day
Won't be enough.

Enough to stop me.

Scared that those fateful times
Will be my downfall.

I am loyal to you.
Because you are you.

But can you blame me,

For being me?

Uncompromising.

This was my world,
But it seemed too small,
I don't want a life —
Where I can't have it all.

The sky is not the limit,
The stars are.
There is no one direction,
Just the right paths.

Follow me will you?
Just trust & believe.
I don't know the way yet,
But at least you'll be with me.

The cure.

I now crave affection,
Not attention.

I have all the love I need from the one
I desire the most.

& yet I don't feel whole,
As this shallow void seems to be growing.

I try to cover it with tape
But the emptiness is so loud,
I can't escape.

Soon I'll learn the only cure is —
Self-love.

After Effect.

I will let you know when I'm free,
& I've recovered from these scars.

I will let you know if it gets any better in here,
When the doubt creeps in but doesn't
Stonewall me —
Anymore.

I will let you know if my hard shell melts a little,
& my heart softens at the sight or thought of you.

My trauma has done a number on me,
But hopefully, you can heal my wounds.

I'm not a narcissist I swear,
Just a victim to one.

I won't let it turn me into one of them,
I won't let them know they've won.

Preservation.

You weren't ready —
For this kind of messy love.

Your innocent heart,
& beautiful soul — yet to be tainted
By an unforgettable heartbreak.

I didn't have it in me to be that for you.

I didn't want to be that for you.

Whilst I was dealing with mine;
I did my best to protect you from yours.

Hopefully,
One day;
When the time is right,
Our hearts will meet again.

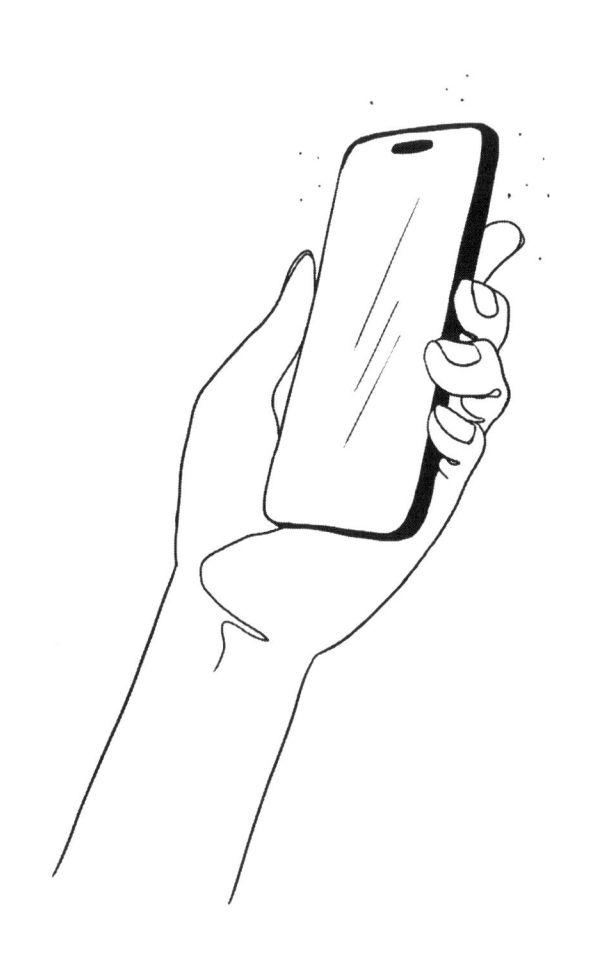

BEST FRIEND?

Noun: A person's closest friend — that may bide their time in the friend zone, knowing that what you share is more than just your interests. You share an underlying love that no one dares to mention. Until one day you do.

1. I'm scared to lose you as my best friend, but life with you would make sense?
2. I love you, but only as a friend.

Memorable.

When you reach this stage of love,
Life won't ever be the same.

Whether it stands the test of time,
Or ends in a tornado.

It will leave an everlasting mark,
One that you will never be able to ignore.

As much as you persist to scrub it out,
Its presence will always make itself known.

Autumn Nights.

If I can't have it back;
I don't want to reminisce.

It only hurts,
With no cause but to remind you
of that empty feeling.
Of guilt,
Loss & —
Longing.

More complex than missing that one person,
More so missing that period of time.

How the air smelt,
How music felt,
How warm our phone calls felt in the cold.

It was a time I will forever miss,
You were a time I could never forget,

No matter how hard I try/tried.
Every autumn, you're in the back of my mind.

Soul-tie.

You finish my sentences,
& burrow into my thoughts.

In a group-wide conversation,
I seek only your answers,
& you look only in my direction —
Prompting my responses,
With jests & light-hearted remarks.

I'm forced to think & dig deeper,
To understand & explain our differences —
Whilst all the while feeling drawn to you.

I long for each of our conversations.

You.

I love you,
I appreciate you,
I want you.

Unanswered.

All these things left unsaid,
We both knew not to say.

Inappropriate?
Unrequited?
Fleeting.

Once you say it, you can't take it back.
All you can do is move on.

If?

If only I had asked you to stay?

If only I had said yes to that date?

If only I had been honest from the start?

If only I had given you a chance?

Misunderstanding.

Sorry that my understanding was
Delayed.

If it were sooner,
Maybe
You
Would
Have
Stayed...

Regret.

I have a you-shaped hole,
That is now filled with regret
Of that moment we crossed the line.

Minimal words exchanged that only
We could read between
The lines.

The very few "I love you's"
I didn't realise —
Actually meant a great deal,
With time.

Final Moments.

She thought that was the last time...

The last time she would feel special.

The last time she would be stopped
In her tracks for a kiss.

The last time she'd look up
& catch him glancing her way.

She cherished each of these moments
As if she knew...

It was the last time.

Expiration.

You know that feeling of awkward silence,
Between two people that were once very fond
Of one another.

The kind of silence that could not be resolved
By just one conversation.
The kind that sounds so empty but is heaving —
With discontent,
Anticipation,
& thousands of words left unsaid.

She was tired of making excuses
& he was tired of trying to understand —
Her,
Them,
Anything.

Their hearts & passions were no longer in sync,
There was *'nothing'* left to fight for.
That was the day,
It was done.

To Reconcile.

I asked to speak to him.

He resisted as expected,
I persisted as planned.

He gave in —
I felt a rush of relief.

"Never meant to hurt or lose you,
It was all my fault."

His eyes softened &
Then he did something
I never anticipated.

Gripped my arm,
Lightly pulled me in close —
For a hug.

"I missed you friend…"

Let go.

I love you too much,
Which is why I have to let you go.

My first love is what you meant to me.

A friend to you is what I'll always be.

You're made for more,
More than my brain could possibly
Comprehend how —
Much.

More —
You'll grow without me,
& that kind of friend I will be.

Starting from now.

FOREVER

Adverb: A connection that will last for an eternity. The most special moments will exist in your heart and memory for all future time.

1. They walked away from one another, knowing that their relationship was not going to last but that their love would be forever.
2. You are my forever love.

Adjective: Lasting or permanent.

Renewed.

I feel as though I was on the brink of death,
& then you saved me.

Thunderstorms.

In your arms for the first time,
Feels familiar.

Like I've known this place forever.

Once spark —
Lighting after the other.

My mind can't keep up.

It's raining outside,
& I'm here in your arms.

This & you —
Feel dangerously perfect.

Remarkable.

Somehow I knew that this was it.
Somehow I knew that you were the one.

That I was going heal with,
Grow with —
Learn to love so deeply.

But it wasn't the right time.

For this to stand the test of time —
We both had to grow through a little pain.

To truly appreciate how remarkable
This kind of love was.

Grateful is an understatement.

Serenity.

The kind of love,
That makes you smile to yourself.

That makes you think of —
The future,
The past,
& the present.

That makes you consider
Nothing,
But feel
Everything.

That grants you peace,
At your most restless moments.

That kind of love.

Bliss.

Surrounded by an abyss of clouds,
As far into the skies as one could possibly imagine.

I place my spoon down after making the most
Perfect cup of tea.

I scroll through the screen & to my surprise,
Discover my favourite albums.

Quite literally in the middle of nowhere.

The lights suddenly dim to a blue mood lighting.
I turn to my left,
& face my favourite human.

Utter contentment.
Utter peace.

A moment created just for me.
Supreme timing.

Eternal.

Attraction is futile,
Connection is forever.

Could be wavering,
Could be weak.

Yet still it remains,
Long after we may part.

Moments may be fleeting,
But this kind of love is forever.

My Favourite Sunset.

Safe with your arms,
Wet with your lips,
Passion becomes me.

Your chest is my home,
Your eyes are gifts.

Like a window overlooking a sunset,
I long to see each day.

Effortless.

He didn't care
What the future held.
All he knew,
In those moments
Was that life made sense
When she was around.
Loving her
Was the easiest, most effortless thing.
"Where did I find you?"
He would say out loud
Quietly thinking
"I don't ever want to lose you".

After You.

My happiest days are when
I am with you,
My happiest moments are when
I feel closest to you.

My saddest days were long before
I met you,
Even if this isn't forever.

I'm glad I experienced all of this
With you.

Day dreamer.

She imagines hundreds of different scenarios
As to how this relationship might turn out.

Granted she cannot
Predict,
Nor will it ever be possible.
To know —
How it will truly unfold.

Live your story,
Stop trying to rewrite it.

I Promise.

If I leave this earth tomorrow,
I want you to know,
That I have loved you
With every part of my being.

There is no room for
Distrust or ego,
But instead - patience & communication.

I do not wish to change you,
I choose to love every stage
Of your *evolution*.

You are my home
& I wish to be yours...

Always.

Truth being,
If I ever had love for you,
I always will.

I cannot hate what I once loved,
No matter how hard I try.

The tears, disappointment, anger,
Frustration, bewilderment
All disintegrate into nothing.

I yearn for peace,
To be left with nothing but fond memories
Of you.

References.

- Young: "Young." (n.d.). In Cambridge English Dictionary. Retrieved from *https://dictionary.cambridge.org/dictionary/english/young#google_vignette*

- Toxic: "Toxic." (n.d.). In Cambridge English Dictionary. Retrieved from *https://dictionary.cambridge.org/dictionary/ english/toxic*

- Narcissistic: Understanding Narcissism. (2022, April). 5 Harsh Truths About Narcissistic Love. Psychology Today. Retrieved from *https://www.psychologytoday.com/gb/blog/understanding-narcissism/202204/5-harsh-truths-aboutnarcissistic-love?amp*

- Best friend: "Best friend." (n.d.). In MerriamWebster.com Dictionary. Retrieved from *https:// www.merriam-webster.com/dictionary/best%20friend*

- Forever: "Forever." (n.d.). In Cambridge EnglishDictionary. Retrieved from *https://dictionary.cambridge.org/dictionary/english/forever*

Mental Health.

We often accept the love we think we deserve. A better you can lead to a better relationship. With self-love existing as the pivotal part.

For those seeking mental health support on their self-love journey, here are some recommendations if you're unsure where to start:

~ Mind
- mind.org.uk
A mental health charity offering advice and support to anyone experiencing a mental health problem. Provides information on dealing with abuse and finding local services.

~ Better Help
- www.betterhelp.com
The world's largest therapy service. 100% online.

~ Therapy Head 2 Heart
- www.therapyhead2heart.com
In Liverpool Street London. Provides you the space you need to invest in you, your healing and your setbacks.

Printed in Great Britain
by Amazon

271b54af-520a-4170-a78f-e8f17fece005R01